STILL FLOWS THE BURNS

STILL FLOWS
THE BURNS

Hugh J. Waters

Keith Murray
PUBLISHING

First published 1992

ISBN 1 870978 50 1

Keith Murray Publishing
46 Portal Crescent
Tillydrone
Aberdeen AB2 2SP

ACKNOWLEDGEMENTS

Cover design by Scott Paton

Illustrations by Sheena Blackhall

Back cover illustration by Muriel Carlaw

Author photograph: Barrhead News

Typeset from disc, prepared by Maggie Seaton,
by Columns Design and Production Services Ltd, Reading

Printed and bound by Mackays of Chatham plc

Wi' a' the time that's left tae me,
Wan thing I'd dae afore I dee;
Tae leave ahint some wark o' fame
That men may read an' ken my name.
Sae speed my pen ower ev'ry page;
As, like a bard frae bygone age,
My songs I sing in words o' rhyme;
A minstrel who's born oot o' time.

H.J.W.

Dedication

To the bravest lass that 'ere I kent –
My wife Patricia

CONTENTS

SUPERFICIAL BURNS . . .

FOREWORD

My dear reader, what you have in your hand is not, nor was it ever intended to be, an anthology of verse compiled for academic study. It is nothing more than a collection of doggerel lines aimed at providing some measure of entertainment for those who like to read; or those who like to listen.

It all began a number of years ago when I was asked by Scottish Television to write one of their annual Burns programmes. The programme, entitled "There was a Lad . . .", starred Kenneth McKellar, with the late Robin Richardson as the narrator. During rehearsals various memos circulated regarding the forthcoming show. Steeped as we were in the Burns cult, the correspondence between the producer and myself gradually developed into rhyme. As rehearsals progressed, so the rhymes got longer and longer in a verbal game of one-upmanship. In an attempt to claim the final victory, I composed an updated version of "Tam o' Shanter" and sent it to the producer, asking for his comments. His reply remains unprintable. "Tam the Bunnet", however, far from being the end of my poetic aspirations, was only the beginning.

I have no doubt that a great many Burns devotees will consider it a gross impertinence on my part for even attempting to emulate the literary standards of our National Bard. Let me assure them right away that no such comparison was ever contemplated. My excursions into the realms of Burns-type verse are based on the premise that "imitation is the sincerest form of flattery". I am convinced that even his most ardent admirer would agree with me that Rab was essentially a writer of his time, committing to verse the happenings and beliefs of his own day and age. What I have done (or attempted to do) is to imagine the type of event or situation which would probably have inspired the ploughman-poet if he had been alive today. Whether or not I have succeeded is something, dear reader, you must judge for yourself.

So much for the motivation, but now a brief explanation of the editorial lay-out of this publication. It is fitting that it should begin with "A Toast to Rab". This particular poem has been recited on many occasions, and I am delighted, and indeed flattered, to report that it has always been given a most enthusiastic reception. In the chapter which follows are a series of poems which are modernised versions of original Burns work. When I say "original" one must, of course, remember that Rab himself repeatedly indulged in the art of re-vamping other people's verses. A qualification of any would-be poet is a penchant towards graffito: Burns himself endorsed this fact with lines scribbled on various objects that ranged from tombstones to church windows. Within this book are a number of short verses scribbled on a number of trappings of life – and death! – in the twentieth century. The final chapter is devoted to poems which are neither parodies nor updated versions of Burns' works. They are, nevertheless, composed in the Burns idiom, some of them even in the famous Burns stanza.

Today, the memory of Robert Burns is etched on the heart of every true Scot. But for him recognition came too late. I mention this sombre fact in the hope of averting the common cliche of history repeating itself. So, should you perchance find any outstanding merit in my humble verse, please do not wait until I am gone and then build my statue at the town centre. Rather send me your donations now while I can still enjoy them.

BY WAY OF AN INTRO . . .

A TOAST TO RAB

"The Star O' Rabbie Burns" . . .
A song, I'm sure, you a' know well;
A song that has a tale to tell.
For it began sae long ago
Beneath a sky of threat'ning snow
When, through the howlin' wind an' sleet,
A new-born babe was heard tae greet.
An' there, it raised its tiny loof
Up tae the thackit cottage roof.
This was a voice soon a' wad ken;
This was a haun' wad wield a pen;
For on that simple Ayrshire child
The great Poetic Muse had smiled,
And, as a Christ'ning Piece, she brung
A thousand songs as yet unsung.

Raised in the lands his father ploughed;
Schooled as their meagre means allowed;
Rab grew in strength and soon in time
His ready wit gave vent in rhyme.
Fast frae his brain the verses spilled,
As fertile as the soil he tilled;
Fast as his plough ower furrows flew,
Yet faster still his poems grew.

Nae knightly deeds his work inspired;
Nae classic themes his spirits fired;
But simple things, and simple ways
Moved him to write his greatest lays.
A cottar, in his humble hoose;
A mountain daisy; an' a moose;
Of Tam o' Shanter's epic ride;
Of toothache; hypocrites an' pride;
Where e'er his fancy would befa',
The Bard immortalised them a';
And, oft a prey tae Cupid's lance,
His heart wad mourn some lost romance.

But yet, for a' he had to give,
Rab struggled for the right to live.
Denied of a' the joys o' wealth;
Restricted by his falt'ring health,
He left, for a' the world tae read
A Treasury o' Verse, indeed.

Sae mony years hae long since past,
Since his great pen was stilled at last.
But time, nor tide, shall never fade
The part that he in history played;
An' faithful, as each year returns
We'll drink this toast: "Tae Rabbie Burns!"

BURNS – PAST AND PRESENT . . .

TAM THE BUNNET
A Modern Tam O' Shanter

That hour when daylicht starts tae fail,
When public works begin tae scale;
The workers hameward wend their way
Content wi' what they've earned that day;
When shoaps draw blin's an' douse the licht,
Their doors a' padloacked snug an' ticht;
'Tis then Hell's Gates are open wide
An' drouthy mooths gan fast inside;
Their haun's an' faces smirched wi' grease;
Their limbs fu' decked in dungarees;
They ca' their roon; they drink it straight;
Let wife, let weans, let supper wait!

Each day when weary toil is through
Ae man was foremost in the queue,
The sale o' drink they'd ne'er begun it,
When through the door came Tam the Bunnet.

Oh, Tam! Wad you but stop tae think
How much you are a slave tae drink!
Time efter time had you been warned,
But sage advice you sneered an' scorned.
You even had been kent tae laugh
When folks ca'ed you, "A Drunken Nyaff"!

Let lesser men collect rare stamps;
Or mess aboot wi' wid an' clamps.
Let others gairden, bool, or fish,
Or paint an' paper if they wish;
Or e'en print photaes in the lobby:
Pubs an' drinkin' was your hoabby!
At hame, your poor demented wife
Had tried tae change your ways o' life,
Wi' anguished heart, oan bended knees,
She'd cry, "Lay aff, afore you get D.T.'s!"

Alas, poor wife, your wisest word
Is ta'en as being quite absurd.
Like seeds that's sowed on rocks they wither;
Gan' in wan ear, an' oot the ither.

But, to our tale:
Ae Friday, on the stroke o' five,
Tam grabbed his pey an' made a dive,
And at the pub, as ae, was first,
Tae cuff his cash an' quench his thirst.
There followed fast upon his heel
A figure that he kent fu' weel:
Wi' ferret face an' middle-shed,
His pal an' confidant, Wee Red.
Wee Red, an expert at the shirkin',
Had swore an oath 'gainst ever workin';
An oath he'd kept fu' staunch an' true —
Twa decades he'd been oan The B'roo.
"Work's for fools!", was Red's avowance,
As he blately drank the Wean's Allowance!

An' so this nicht found Red an' Tam
Together oan their nightly dram.

The clock sped oan wi' warning tick,
But Tam, he didnae care a "Hic".
Wee Red was pourin' in his lugs
Excitin' tales o' racin' dugs.
They'd drink as long as they were able . . .!
Syne they wad meet ablow the table!

But 'tho some hoors we live sublime,
Nae man can ever harness time,
Nae maitter hoo we try tae jouk it,
Tempus still will always fugit.
An', even 'tho he lo'ed the stuff,
Tam soon jaloused he'd had enough.
Through a' his veins the whisky veered;
It slurred his speech; his sicht it bleared;
The flair beneath him seemed tae stoat,
Like purridge, bilin' in a poat.
But what had happened worst of a',
Where Red had stood . . . there now stood twa!
On rubber legs Tam crossed the floor
An' passed oot through the swingin' door.

Ootside the storm was at its hicht –
It was a real Scotch Summer's nicht –
The wind it blew as if tae tak
The shirt an' waistcoat aff your back;
The icy-cauld, torrential rains

Were fast o'erflowin' protestin' drains.
Ahint the pub, against the dyke,
Tam found his rusty, trusty bike
An' soon was fleein' through mud an' mire
Tae hame an' supper by the fire.

Let wind and watter dae its worst;
Tam pedalled oan and mildly cursed;
The whisky warm within him glowed,
"I dinnae gie a damn it snowed!"
Like athlete strivin' for a medal
He turned an unrelenting pedal.
The bike flew ower the ancient streets,
Past polis oan their night-shift beats;
Fish-supper shoaps, wi' greasy wares;
Past couples winchin' oan the stairs;
Past news-boys, cuttin' fancy capers
As they tried tae flog the next day's papers.
Ignorin' a' the passin' sights –
Ignorin' a' the traffic lights –
Tam raced his rubber-tyred wheels
As if Auld Nick was oan his heels.
Nae thocht had he o' oany kind
As busy toon he left behind
An' sped alang the country road
That led him tae his ain abode.
Aboot him a' was drab an' bare
As he approached dread "Jile Square"!
Noo on this spot, in years gone by,
Rogues an' thieves hung oot tae die!
Nae man in sober sense or sane,
This haunted road wad e'er hae ta'en.

But Tam – wi' whisky-fuddled heid –
Feared not the livin' or the deid!
Against the stories auld wives cried
Brave Tam was duly fortified.
Ghaists an' boggles an' the like
Wad never catch him oan his bike.
Besides, nae spirits he presumed
Could match the spirits he'd consumed!

But as he pedalled through the nicht,
The place aroon' was bathed in licht.
Frae ower the thorny hedge o' whin
There came a hellish, heathen din.
Poor Tam wi' fricht near drappit deid,
The hair it curled upon his heid,
His face turned tae an ashen hue,
For there, before his very view,
A sicht as ne'er by mortal seen;
He scarcely could believe his een!

Noo just imagine if you can
On every dance conceived by man,
But leapin', loupin', loathsome prancers,
Instead o' lichtsome, lithesome dancers.
Well, this Tam saw tae his dismay.
His courage quickly drained away
An' there he stood an' quaked wi' fear . . .
Nae mortal getherin' was here!
He eyed the dancers wan by wan,
As doon his spine the cauld sweat ran.

A bookie who had run away,
Six favourites had won that day,
Was loupin' there withoot his trews,
An' oan his feet were horses' shoes!
A factor who'd dae nae repair
Tae oany hoose within his care,
Was bein' burled aff his feet
By a wife he'd thrown intae the street!
An' ower there twa weel-kent lugs,
Who'd made a fortune dopin' dugs;
Wi' whup in paw an ootsized hare
Was chasin' this exhausted pair.
Anither yin was Sleekit Sanny;
A spiled boy who'd slashed his granny!
They hooched, they reeled, they pas-de-barred;
Oan pairtners' toes they came doon hard,
Watched ower by Musical Director –
A wan-time Income Tax Inspector.

Tam stood like wan who'd been entranced,
An' roon aboot the shower glanced.
The piper struck anither tune
An' wan an' a' went prancin' roon.
'Twas then the piper Tam could see –
A Polis Sergeant, R.I.P.;
The wan who'd lifted Tam an' a';
For thingummying against a wa'!

Wi' muckle zest an' frantic squeals
They danced their complicated reels.
Their legs an' airms wi' vicious swipes

Cleft air in timin' tae the pipes.
They worked themselves tae frantic state
As faster, faster grew the rate.
Depravity stamped every face;
This was the scum o' the human race!
Hoodlums, wasters, pimps an' tramps,
Gangsters, mobsters, shysters, scamps,
Rogues and thieves – and worse tae tell –
Drunkards; just like Tam, himsel'!

The music suddenly crescendit,
Tam thocht, "The dancin' must be ended!"
For a' the mob cavortin' there
Withdrew an' left the centre bare;
An' where before had been elation,
There cam an air o' expectation.
The piper paused one breath; no more.
Then stertit louder than before,
An' frae the throats o' a' an' sundry
There cam a murmur, rollin', thund'ry.
Oot there trouped, oan legs like stilts,
Five gill boattles dressed in kilts!
In time tae piper's furious tune
They startit bobbin' up an' doon;
Like livin' things they pranced aboot,
'Til a' their coarks cam poppin' oot:
An' precious whisky they'd confined
Was back tae Mither Earth consigned!

Poor Tam, before he'd never faced
Such flagrant, wanton, dire waste.

His very soul he'd gladly truck
For what was spillin' ower the muck!
Before he could his thochts repair
Anither dancer took the flair
An' by the cheer from fearful faction
This surely was the star attraction!
Tam's een stuck oot like organ stops,
For there, daein' cantrips, jives an' hops
Was his sworn enemy of a'
Auld "Hatchet Face"; his mother-in-law!
She kicked an' flung in acrobatics;
Gone was her stiffness, her rheumatics!

In mony verbal battles lost
His mother-in-law poor Tam had crossed;
Mony a time in black despair
He'd felt like throwin' her doon the stair.
But still, tonight his ain wife's maw
Surpassed herself abune them a';
Repentance flowed, Tam gi'ed a yell,
"That's it, Auld Yin, gaun yersel'!"

The music ceased! The lichts went oot!
Then efter Tam in hot pursuit,
The devilish horde, wi' dev'lish speed,
Cam oan . . . Big Bella in the lead!
Tam leapt his bike, the wheels he spun,
An' left like bullet frae a gun.
Ae thocht was foremost in his mind
Tae jouk the roarin' mob behind.

CAIRRY OOT

An' if his win' could last the pace,
Then Tam, he knew the very place:
Some twa miles doon the road an Inn
Which if he passed he knew he'd win,
For Bella-o-the-Thursty-Gub
Had ne'er been known tae pass a pub!

The spokes grew rid-hoat on the wheels;
The mob pressed hard upon his heels,
An' just when Tam nae mair could try,
His hallowed spot, the pub, flew by!
Big Bella gi'ed ae desperate snatch,
But Tammie's jaicket couldnae catch;
So he escaped the savage cratur . . .
But left ahint his tyre inflator!

This tale is true; its moral's clear:
If you drink whisky, gin, or beer,
Whene'er you feel your thirst is slaked,
Lay aff afore you get hauf jaked!
Remember Shanter's mare's bald rump;
Remember Tam the Bunnet's pump!
An' should you drink oan at this juncture . . .
God help you if you have a puncture.

TO A FISH SUPPER
(Our Other National Dish)

Oh thou, the feast o' modern livin',
As wance the manna doon frae Heaven
Appeased the host frae bondage driven;
    An' greased their belly.
So now art thou tae mankin' given,
    Thou morsel smelly!

Nae mortal chef thy form designed.
Your birth was of a nobler kind.
Perhaps in Heaven where angels dined,
    You first saw light;
And in The Golden Book was signed:
    "We're fryin' tonight!"

When Damocles his hunger fed,
Ignoring that above his head,
Which held his life in spid'ry thread,
    He danger spurned;
And on thy welcome sight instead
    His eyes he turned.

Before the pow'r o' Rome was halted
The Emperors, Divine, Exalted;
In dining halls o' marble vaulted,
    Kent weel thy fare.
They ate until their guts revolted,
    Then asked for mair!

When Raleigh came to Englan's shore
Wi' treasures never seen before,
His name was famed for evermore
    For in his ships,
He brought the plants we a' adore –
    Turned intae chips.

In cooncil hoose or lord's estate,
In paper poke or cheeny plate,
Your welcome sight we contemplate,
    Tae tempt oor swallies.
While in atween each bite we state:
    "God bless The Tallies!"

THE TWA DUGS

A wee dug snowkit roon a bin,
To see what treasures lay within –
Some scraps o' meat by men despised
Are in the duggy world much prized!
And as he prowled wi' senses keen,
Anither tyke came on the scene.

Here was a noble dug indeed –
A "Caesar" o' the canine breed! –
The outward four-legged indication
O' his maister's high, exalted station;
An immigrant tae Scotland's shore,
Imported mony years before.
The glitterin' band his neck caressed
Shewed he was used tae ha'ein' the best.
But pride o' station, nane had he.
A hint o' sadness tinged his e'e;
And in his sorry, soleful stare
He craved the freedom he should share;
Tae run an' play, or to engage,
Wi' tykes o' doubtful parentage;
Tae sniff each gatepost he should see,
Or lift his leg 'gainst every tree.
The ither mutt that made the pair
Was of a species very rare.
Nae man could say where he'd been sired;

32

His mither's morals nane enquired.
His ugly, shaggy, mis-shaped heid
Made him the mongrel thoroughbreid!
     But what, in looks, this dug had missed
Were made up by a nature blest,
For lads and lassies, men and wife
Had found in "Luath" a freen' for life.
A kindly pat; a scrap o' meat;
In pub or playground, shoap or street –
This was the life this tyke had won;
A freen' tae a', but slave tae none!
     An' so these twa they cam' thegither,
An' baith sat doon tae hae a blether . . .
But first – afore they tak' their ease –
They must exchange their curtesies.
Inherent manners a'e prevail
So introductions, head to tail,
Soon break the bonds and set them free
From the fetters o' formality.
So, having saved the situation,
Their thochts now turn to conversation.

CAESAR

     Freen', Luath, can you please explain
A thocht that's always wracked my brain.
How, in the name o' a' alive,
Dae poor dugs manage tae survive?
     My maister's in the upper-brackets;
Mixed up in lots o' different rackets;
Wi' loads o' flunkies a'e oan hand –
His every wish is their command:

33

"Bring roon' my Rolls!"; "Leave oot my suit!";
"Make sure my clubs are in the boot!".
Whatever pleasures man can claim
Are bought wi' cheques that bear his name.
      We have a kitchen staff alone
Who work their fingers tae the bone.
The likes o' this you've never seen.
It's like a bloody works canteen!
There's a' sorts o' exotic dishes,
Frae plates o' saps tae biled fishes . . .
An' everybody gets their fill,
An' when that's done there's plenty still.
The chars that even wash the stairs
Are wined and dined like millionaires!
Quite frankly, Luath, it's got me beat
What folks in Cooncil Hooses eat.

LUATH

      Aye, Caesar, there's no doubt it's true,
The likes o' us don't live like you.
An' whiles it's nearly got us beat –
The way tae mak the baith en's meet –
But even so we struggle oan,
An' somehow manage tae keep goin'.
It's folks like us appreciate
The joys o' bein' a Welfare State.
      For even 'tho' you're unemployed
There's still nae need tae be annoyed;
The Great Provider sees you through –
A thing we poor folks ca' The B'roo!
Aye, mony a faimily's been reared,

34

An' frae the pangs o' hunger spared
Withoot daein' work o' oany kin',
Save, signin' oan the dotted line!

CAESAR

But surely poor folks o' the nation
Must live a life o' dire frustration?
The upper-class don't care a hoot
What ploys the masses are aboot.
You only live, as I can see,
For tasks ablow their dignity.
On top o' that, it's safe tae bet,
You live in constant fear o' debt!
For every pound you earn it seems,
You owe the hauf oan Purchase Schemes.
An', sure as Fate, there comes a day
When you've bought mair than you can pay;
When scant possessions you've acquired
Are sold tae meet the cash required.
You ca' that life! 'Pon my heid,
You'd be a damned sight happier deid!

LUATH

Of course, afore you judge oor kin',
You've got tae keep an open min'.
While bein' deprived, to you, looks bad
We don't miss what we've never had.
The standard that we have acquired –
'Tho leavin' much tae be desired –

35

Can be maintained throughout our lives,
By workin' men an' workin' wives.
    An' even when wi' weans we're blessed
Their scanty needs are hardly missed.
Besides, before they even walk or creep,
They're earnin' cash tae pey their keep.
    An' if at times we are depressed,
There's wan sure cure beats a' the rest;
A gless of wine, or swig o' beer,
An' a' oor worries disappear:
Oor min's soar tae a higher plane;
Oor worth as critics quickly gain
As rapidly we mount attacks
On Church, on State, on Income Tax!
    Of course, we've other outlets tae,
To keep our cares an' woes at bay.
A scheme o' pastimes we've designed,
Tae ease the strain on poor mankind.
There's Bingo! Fitba! Television! . . .
A Trinity beyond derision!
    An' as from month tae month we glide
There's special days we've set aside
An', on some pretext or anither,
We join in merriment thegither.
Like Easter-time, or Hallowe'en –
Wi' twa weeks Summer Holidays atween –
An' then, of course, we've Hogmanay,
Tae start oor year wi' revelry.
    But still, for a' these celebrations,
You're right tae think there are occasions
When life among the working nation
Is naught but drudge and dire frustration.
Just think how low oor spirits sink

Each time the telly's oan the blink;
Or how depressed a man can be
Tae hear, "You've failed your M.O.T."
An' 'though it's times like this we dread,
We wait in hope what lies ahead.

CAESAR

Freen', Luath, I hate tae spile your dreams,
But you've nae place in future schemes.
The powers-that-be hae nae set plan
Tae ease the lot o' workin' man.
They gi'e you not a second thought;
Unless, of course, they need your vote.
When that time comes they'll knock your door;
They'll mak you promises galore.
They'll claim their Party is the best
Tae keep you fed an' proper dressed.
They'll talk to you o' this an' that;
They'll gi'e the weans a friendly pat;
They'll ca' you by your Christian name,
An' swear your welfare is their aim.
A life o' leisure yours can be
If they're returned as your M.P.
Wi' glibness few can seldom match,
They bait their lines an' land their catch;
For canvassing for your support,
Tae them is little mair than sport.
You take my word, for I can bet
They'll soon forget you ever met!

LUATH

I quite believe the things you say.
But then, it's always been that way.
There's nae depth tae the rotten tricks
The upper class ca' politics.
     Whatever party comes tae power
They hae nae sooner taken ower
When they are warnin' a' the nation
Aboot the dangers o' Inflation . . .
An evil they will cure in stages,
By extra tax an' "freezin'" wages!
     Then, as the cost o' livin' soars,
The Opposition rants an' roars;
While secretly they a' acclaim,
Were they in power they'd dae the same.
     The mair their fame and fortunes spread
The mair they want tae forge ahead.
But yet, for a' the wealth they've got
They seem a maist unhappy lot!

CAESAR

You never spoke a truer word.
The way they live is quite absurd.
     In spite o' a' their airs an' graces;
Their modern dress an' made-up faces;
These earthly trappings scarce can hide
The turmoil that goes on inside.
Full well they ken their approbation
Could bear but scant investigation.
Tae fin' new pleasures they're obsessed;

An', findin' nane, they're sair depressed;
Then, soon or late, they're specialising
On drink, or drugs, or womanising.
They've nae respect for married life –
The reason why divorce is rife –
At every turn they seize their chance
Tae change their partners, like a dance!
It's difficult to keep ahead
Of who is sleepin' in whose bed!
Love, or lust, whate'er it be,
It earns them mony a braw bawbee,
By boastin' o' romantic capers
In the centre-page o' Sunday papers!
An' if by chance should kids appear –
Imposing sanctions maist severe –
They solve this problem, as a rule,
By sending them tae Boarding School.
      This action leaves them free tae boast
How much their education cost;
For, in their ain misguided way,
They gauge things by how much you pay.
      Some poor folks think it is a must
Tae emulate the upper-crust,
But, from experience I've acquired,
There's little there tae be desired.
The Good Life's far from what it seems;
A world o' excess and extremes;
Morals an' scruples play no part
In climbin' up the social chart;
An' havin' reached the dizzy height
They soon forget those still in plight.
      There are a few whose slates are clean,
But they are few an' far between.

At this the dugs got tae their feet,
Preparing for a quick retreat,
For they'd espied a gang o' weans
Armed tae the teeth wi' sticks an' stanes.
Says Luath, "The younger generation
Give ample theme for conversation,
A topic we must bear in min'
When next we meet, for auld lang syne!"

GREEN GROW THE RASHES, O
(Sung to the Tune of the Original)

This age when wealth is gauged by pow'r,
By wars and bluidy clashes, o
When man at fellow man must glow'r;
They think no' o' the lasses, o.

CHORUS   Green grow the rashes, o
               Green grow the rashes, o
               The sweetest hours that e'er I spent,
               Were spent amang the lasses, o.

They dream o' bombs an' war machines;
They dream o' conquered nations, o;
But spare nae thocht for Nature's queens,
Or their exalted stations, o.

CHORUS

Wi' sick'ning pace the nations race,
Tae conquer stars abune them, o.
But lasses' eyes outshine the skies —
Especially when we lo'e them, o.

41

CHORUS

There's mony a pleasure I hae shared,
O' which I hae repented, o.
But lasses, be the death o' me
An' I will die contented, o.

CHORUS

Wan thing alane mak's me complain,
Wi' every hour that passes, o;
In modern dress it's hard to guess
Just which wans are the lasses, o!

CHORUS

A NED'S PRAYER

(The inner thoughts of an habitual young criminal as he
stands in the dock awaiting the return of the Jury with yet
another "Guilty" verdict.)

Oh, Lord in Heaven – if Lord there be –
Who thinks aboot the likes o' me,
Then on this Courtroom cast thy e'e,
 Almighty Judge;
For a' the world has turned on me
 A vicious grudge.

They envy me my well-kept hair.
They envy me the claes I wear.
Lord, can I help if I've a flair
 For bein' dapper.
Their jealousy drives them, I'll swear,
 Clean aff their napper.

Before that I could even walk;
Before I'd even learned tae talk,
The neighbours livin' in oor block,
 Like spaewives vile,
Had forecast I'd end up in dock,
 An' then the jile.

An' a' because an aunt uncouth
Her finger stuck intae my mooth
Wi' nosey plea, "Let's feel this tooth!"
    Her wish I granted.
I bit wi' a' the verve o' youth.
    That's what she wanted!

Then at school I was abused,
By a' the teachin' staff accused,
Because the belt I wance refused;
    Lord, I was framed
When stink-bombs in the class were used,
    An' I was blamed.

Surrounded as I was by cranks,
Who frowned on a' my boyish pranks –
Like sniffin' glue an' robbin' banks –
    So I became
An outcast from the social ranks;
    Am I to blame?

Each mother warned her wayward son,
My friendship was a thing tae shun,
An' swore that some day I'd be done
    For some foul deed.
I topped the charts as Number One –
    For Peterheid!

Thus was my future life ordained;
My public image waxed an' waned;
Until the Children's Panel proclaimed
    An Institution
Where I would be by law detained,
    Was their solution.

And there, among my fellow peers,
I spent the next five happy years,
Discussin' get-rich-quick careers,
    An' various ploys;
A giant step tae new frontiers –
    Wan o' the boys!

But even here my fate was sealed;
The screws, wi' malice unconcealed,
Their wicked plot tae me revealed
    (A cruel decision)
I'd play the haun' I had been dealed
    Withoot remission!

But even so there came the day
When I rejoined Society
Determined that I'd make them pay
    A heavy cost,
For a' the time I'd been away;
    The years I'd lost.

A plan o' action I'd designed,
Tae reek revenge on a' mankind;
My every move they had maligned,
      An' just because,
I wouldnae let them clog my mind
      Wi' petty laws.

'Twas then, Lord, I began for real
Tae rob an' cheat; tae thieve an' steal;
An' yet, nae scruples did I feel'
      Nae deep regret;
I'd make the public squirm an' squeal
      Tae square my debt.

The mony talents I possess
Made my task almost effortless,
I planned each job wi' thoroughness
      Tae fetch mair skin.
The polis tried wi' nae success
      Tae run me in.

Alas, wan night when I was oot
I came across this daft galoot,
Who said he'd train me how tae shoot,
      An' then I'd be
A man tae fear withoot a doot;
      He'd guarantee!

So, just tae hae a bit o' fun,
I soon acquired a sawn-off gun . . .
That's when my troubles a' begun;
    I'd live tae rue it.
A "shooter" is a thing tae shun,
    Had I but knew it.

I had a nice wee scheme on hand –
A job I had already planned –
I reckoned ten or twenty grand
    It wad entail;
An' wi' a gun at my command,
    How could it fail!

But in that plan there was a flaw;
Some bastard shopped me tae the law
Who come an' cairted me awa' –
    The Fascist scum –
They swore they'd stick me ower the wa'
    For years to come.

An' so, Dear Lord, it's up tae you,
For a' the hassle I've been through
I hope you'll see my point of view;
    On my behalf,
If you could pu' a string or two,
    You'd get me aff!

LINES SCRIBBLED . . .

ON THE HEADSTONE OF A DEPARTED GIRLFRIEND

Tae Bonnie Jean – A Queen o' Wimmen.
Alas! She overdone the slimmin'.

ON THE TOMBSTONE OF A DEAD NEIGHBOUR

A bilin' kettle brought the end
Of this, our maist esteamed friend.

ON THE GRAVE OF A DEAD MOTORIST

You proved to us in life, Tam,
That you had what it takes.
You proved to us in death, Tam,
Your caur had faulty brakes!

ON THE TOMBSTONE OF A DEAD WORKMATE

Tae Wull, who's left us a' ahint.
It's no' the first time Wull's been skint.
Where'er he wanders all alone,
We pray he's in a smokeless zone.

ON THE GRAVESTONE OF A DEAD CELT

Discretion's Valour's next-of-kin;
So don't throw Caution tae the win'.
But cherish, like a virtue, Fear;
Or else your bones, like mine, lie here!
Oh, would I never, for a lark,
Sung "Bless the Pope" – in Ibrox Park!

ON A BLOOD TRANSFUSION POSTER

Scots wha' hae wi' Wallace bled,
        Wance mair your country's in the red;
Sae save the gore that wance you shed
        'Gainst foreign foes' intrusions.
Like thrifty sons, bank it instead;
        It's needed for Transfusions.

ON A NEWSPAPER PLACARD ANNOUNCING THE LASTEST SPACESHOT

If there be life abune the stars;
If man exists on Moon or Mars;
I see nae reason why that we
Are no' content tae let them be.
So let us leave them tae their ain,
For knowing us they've naught tae gain,
Oor presence there wad implement
An inter-planet discontent.
Besides, we've surely now been taught,
We cannae rule the world we've got!

ON THE BACK OF A MEDICAL PRESCRIPTION

We've pills tae mak us sleep at night;
We've pills tae stay awake;
We've even pills tae cure the ills
Of other pills we take.
We've pills tae stop a wean bein' born;
We've pills tae keep us thin;
We've pills tae build us up again,
Or cure a scabby chin.
We've pills tae mak us placid, calm;
We've pills tae mak us brave;
We've pills that mak us quiet;
An' pills that mak us rave.
In every day, in every way,
We've pills tae face life's battle;
It's comin' soon, as we walk roon,
I'm sure you'll hear us rattle!

ON A C.N.D. POSTER

Let nae man question how I feel,
Or be in doobt about my zeal;
The "Bomb" I violently oppose,
An' I'm prepared to jine wi' those
Who in their various demonstrations
Condemn atomic-weapon nations.
I'll haun' oot tracts; I'll white-wash wa's,
Tae draw attention tae oor cause.
I'll jine in marches; sign petitions;
I'll even heckle politicians.
Wan thing alane wad mak me quit;

53

On pavements hard I will not sit!
It's no that I've a fear o' jiles;
But oh, it's murder on the piles!

ON AN H.P. AGREEMENT FORM

If there's a vice, that's worse by twice,
Than staunin' in a pub, man,
Then list tae me, an' you'll agree,
It's dealin' wi' a clubman.

If there's a name the De'il can claim,
Then surely you can bet, man,
It's on the line on which we sign
For oany kin' o' debt, man.

If there's a scourge, which we should purge;
A plague that really herms, man,
God gi'es the will tae cure the ill
That we ca' Credit Terms, man.

If you are sane, then to remain
Outwith the realms o' fey, man,
Beware the snare that's everywhere —
Just buy what you can pay, man!

SUPERFICIAL BURNS . . .

The Lassies oh!

THE LASSIES

When God this troubled world began,
In His great mind He had a plan
Tae mak a place where beast an' man
    Could live an' share,
In peace an' harmony as wan;
    Withoot a care.

Then Adam o'er this vast domain,
As king of all was sent tae reign;
Withoot the need tae sweat or strain
    Tae prove his might,
Until, fed up wi' bein' alane,
    He prayed ae night:

"Dear Lord, each creature you've created
Has grown in strength, has wo'ed an' mated;
Whilst I alane remain frustrated –
    Nae love ha'e I.
My loneliness must be abated,
    Or let me die!"

What then befell is common lore;
A rib frae Adam's side He tore;
He breathed on it, wan breath no more;
    An' there she stood;
A gift frae Heaven's Treasure Store –
    Sweet womanhood!

An' thus in Eden there was made
The endless match 'twixt man an' maid;
An', side by side, their paths were laid
    For good or ill.
The laws o' love that they obeyed
    The world would fill.

Since then, of course, it's nae surprise,
Man views the world through Adam's eyes.
Wi' a' the wiles he can devise
    He plans his life,
Tae share his earthly Paradise
    Wi' his braw wife.

A world o' men, we'll a' agree,
A melancholy place wad be
Wi' nae fair maids for company:
    How we wad miss them!
So raise your glass an' toast wi' me:
    "The Lassies – Bless Them!"

THE ITHER DRIVER

Where are you gaun, you bluidy fool!
It's folk like you who as a rule
Can heap the coals o' ridicule
    Oan a' who drive.
Awa' back tae the Learner's School –
    An' stey alive!

For three miles noo I've watched you playin'
At hoppin' oot an' in each lane,
Like some demented, stupid wean
    Who goes a binder,
Each time that he's let oot alane –
    Withoot a minder.

Three times you've raced the amber light;
You've signalled Left when turnin' Right;
A cyclist nearly died o' fright
    When you flashed past.
I'm sure you must be short o' sight;
    Or else hauf gassed!

'I telt ye it didna say car park!!'

You'd think when travellin' through a toon
You'd try at least tae slow it doon;
But naw! Your fit remains pressed doon
    Flat wi' the flair.
I'll bet your speedo points abune
    A ton, or mair.

It's clowns like you who bring disaster,
Because your lust you cannae master
Tae travel faster, faster, faster!
    So keep the heid;
Or soon you'll be encased in plaster –
    Or even deid!

Anither thing I fail tae see,
How you got through an M.O.T.;
Your caur's as rusty as can be –
    A load o' scrap!
Apart frae that, take it frae me,
    Your drivin's crap!

I think you've really had it noo,
For I can see the boys in blue –
Wi' flashin' lights an' sirens too –
    Alang the road . . .
But wait! It's *me* they want tae interview . . .
    Ah help my Goad!

WULL THE WASTER

He ran alang demented,
He was nearly oot his mind,
His coat was wildly flappin'
An' fleein' oot behind.
Through sweat-bleared e'en alang the street
He cast a hurried glance,
To where his bus – the last that night –
Was waitin' at the stance.
His elbows pounded on his ribs,
His legs like pistons thrust.
It seemed his lungs were fu' o' san'
An' ready for tae burst.
There was a time when sich a dash
Would just hae made him grin,
But, like a thief, strong drink an' fags
Had robbed him o' his win'.

Oh, Wull, had you but listened mair
When sage advice was given;
Had you ne'er ta'en the weel-paved road
That leads to Easy Livin';
But trod the narrow, staney path
In search o' life's great treasures . . .
What made you turn, as turn you did,
In quest o' wanton pleasures?

A boattle was your dearest freen' –
Afore a' it came first –
It gave you courage; loused your tongue;
An' quenched your burnin' thirst!
Your greatest gift was gamblin',
A talent you acquired,
An' Easy Money was the creed
That a' your life inspired!

Ambition? Well, you'd loads o' that;
Tae live a life o' ease;
Tae ca' nae man your Maister;
An' be idle if you please!
Nae time had you tae work or slave,
For you had lots tae do;
You had your dugs, your fitba' pools,
An' signin' oan the B'roo.
Time was too good tae waste on toil,
You had your pals tae meet;
Tae criticise The Cooncil;
An' tae lounge aboot the street.
You had tae pick your hoarses,
An' wage war oan every boss,
Tae poke fun at The Polis,
An' tae play at Pitch an' Toss.
You had a wife an' three sma' weans,
Sae lovable an' braw,
But time or money spent on them
Was pleasure thrown awa'!
Amang the Neds, you ca'd your pals,
You were a king o' men,
But very near a stranger
In your ain bit but an' ben.

The gap 'tween man an' bus grew less,
Success seemed his tae claim,
Anither tortured burst o' speed
An' he'd be drivin' hame.
Alas, Success – like wimmin folk –
Is fickle and unfair
For in a flash her smile can turn
Tae a cauld and icy stare.

An' just as Wull made up his min',
He'd make it efter a',
Amidst a blast o' diesel fumes
The last bus pu'd awa'!
An' as the tail-light disappeared
Intae the dark o' night
Wull gi'ed a curse for he was in
A maist unhappy plight.
Too long he revelled wi' his pals;
Too swift the time had flown,
An' noo he faced a five-mile walk
Doon country roads, alone!
The thocht o' trudgin' a' that stretch
Was far frae Wullie's likin',
For what he hated maist of a'
Was oany form o' hikin'.
The walk itself was bad enough –
An' ample theme for cursin' –
But the weather it was turnin' bad;
An' threatenin' tae worsen!

An' so a maist unhappy Wull,
Oan maist unsteady feet,
Set oot wi' totterin', falterin' steps
Tae trek his five-mile beat.
The storm set in wi' real intent,
The wind a tempest blew;
For every yaird that Wull advanced
It cairried him back two.
The rain streamed like a cataract
That ower a mountain spews,
It ran doon Wullie's troosers
An' filled his pointed shoes,
But onwards, onwards he advanced
In spite o' Nature's wiles,
Until he'd covered in his strides
A distance o' three miles.

The rain dripped aff his bunnet skip
An' slithered doon his nose;
The icy chill o' sodden claes
His very marrow froze.
But shelter loomed afore his e'en.
He'd staun' ablow yon brig,
Tae catch his breath an' smoke a fag,
An' ha'e a quiet swig;
For in the poacket o' his coat
There hung a welcome weight;
His cairry-oot wad soon relieve
The misery o' his state.
A bevvy is the very thing
Tae boost a man's resistance . . .
But wait! That noise above the storm?

A rumblin' in the distance!
He listened maist intently
As the noise in volume grew,
Then grinned – nae mair he'd have tae walk –
For weel the sound he knew.
He could have jumped for very joy,
Sae great was his elation,
As soon he spied, advancin' fast,
Some form o' transportation.

He waved his bunnet in the air,
"Hey, gi'es a lift!" he cried,
An' heard the screech o' slitherin' wheels
As brakes were fast applied.
It was a bus o' strange design.
The paint was jettest black.
Its lights gi'ed oot an eerie glow,
An' flames flew oot the back.
He couldnae see the inside weel,
For it was deepest gloom.
The number plates at back an' front
Spelled oot the word o' DOOM!
Withoot a sound the door slid back,
An' Wullie skipped aboard.
The bus moved off. The door slammed shut.
Ootside the storm roared.
He rubbed the water frae his e'en.
He shook his drippin' coat.
He looked inside the gloomy bus.
A scream died in his throat!
In every seat a figure sat,
A figure o' despair;

But what shook Wull, 'twas a' his pals
That sat wi' vacant stare.

Fat Jeemie Dodds, a polis nark,
Who ratted on his brither,
An' every Friday night got tight
An' knocked Hell oot his mither.
Wee Ned Dundas, a drunken bum
Who liked to boast an' brag
Of how he'd swiped the pension
Oot his blin' auld auntie's bag.
Big Don M'Turk, the Highlander –
The boys a' ca'd him Kiltie –
Three times they'd charged him wi' assault;
Three times they'd found him guilty.
And there, of course, was Sailor Smith,
Who'd mairrit fourteen times;
Had sunk three boats; an' smuggled dope;
An' superficial crimes.
Rab the Rat – who seldom washed –
An' thocht that he was gifted,
Because he'd kicked a bloke tae death
An' never had been lifted.
An' Stilty Jones, an' Joe the Wop,
An' "Blinkin' Tam" M'Ginney,
An' Taffy Barnes, who just last week
Had been inside Barlinnie.
A' Wullie's pals were gathered there,
A loathsome congregation;
The sweepin's o' the human race
You find in every nation!
Nae glint o' recognition showed,

An' not a word was spoken.
Wull swallied hard an' tried tae grin.
Was this some kind o' jokin'?
But yet his flesh began tae creep.
His hair tae staun' oan end.
The vacant stares; the glassy e'en,
He couldnae comprehend.

A skinny haun' his shoother tapped.
He spun upon his heel.
An' there ahint anither stood,
That Wullie kent fu' weel.
The look o' everlastin' pain
That stamped that face sae vile,
The eyes that burned like red-hoat coals,
The evil, bestial smile.
The yellow, pointed, slaverin' fangs
That crunched an' ground wi' hate,
The horns, the tail, the cloven hooves;
Nae man could imitate!

His finger thrust before Wull's face,
Like talon efter prey.
Wull tried tae move, but terror-struck,
His feet would not obey.
"What dae you want wi' me?" he moaned,
"Just stoap an' let me aff!"
The evil grin was broadened to
A mocking, hollow laugh,
"Och, come noo, Wull, we've just but met,
Why should I let you gang?
Besides, we're goin' to a place,

A place we baith belang!
You've lived a life o' idle ease,
Enjoyed the world's desires;
You've past the test that leads tae rest
In everlastin' fires!"
Wi' heartfelt sobs that shook his frame
Wull drapped oan bended knees
An' long an' hard harangued the De'il
Wi' solemn, hopeless pleas,
"Just wan mair chance tae men' my ways.
I know I've been a flop!
But bell the driver o' the bus;
Command him for tae stop!"
"The same auld story," sneered the De'il,
"Lay aff your whinin' fuss.
'Tis you, my freen', should ken fu' weel
There's naebuddy drives this bus!
When travellin' oan the road o' sin
That leads a man tae Hell
You need nae driver at the wheel,
It's you that drives yoursel'!"

Wull grovelled oan the filthy flair
An' bubbled like a wean;
His hoose, his wife, his faimily,
He'd never see again.
He only had himself tae blame,
The good times he had prized,
Had brought aboot his sorry end;
Had he but realised!
Then suddenly there came a calm,
The win' nae longer sighed;

The icy rain had ceased tae fa';
Ootside, the storm had died!
And through a hole in torn clouds
The moon had seized her chance
Tae bathe the night in silv'ry light
An' Nature's work enhance.
It showed the stately, drippin' trees;
The grasses an' the moss;
It lit the road afore the bus
In one gigantic cross!
The De'il let oot an anguished scream
Wi' pain his face was drawn;
The vision o' that hated cross
He dare not gaze upon.
He dived for cover frae its sight.
The bus came to a halt,
An' Wull was thrown against the door
Wi' sich a sickenin' jolt.
Wi' tremblin' haun's he pu'd the catch,
The door he gave a wrench,
An' flung himsel' frae aff that bus
Intae a wayside trench . . .

An' there Wull lay an' prayed aloud
Upon the marshy ground;
Then, strugglin' frae his hidin' place,
He had a look around.
Of bus, or De'il, or wastrel pals
There wasnae oany sign –
But, oh the memory o' this night
Would never leave his mind!

Weel! that's the tale; the rest you'll guess;
It's no' my joab tae preach;
But true or false, what e'er it be,
There's somethin' here for each.
Like Wull, we're a' inclined tae seek
What pleasures life advances;
But, unlike Wull, there's few o' us
Get oany second chances!

WHEESHT!

When length'ning shadows close the day,
An' drowsy bairnies leave their play;
Deserted noo the nursery stands,
Like new-forsaken Fairy Lands.
The lonely toys their vigils keep
While youthful owners rest an' sleep.

A wee sma' voice tae Heaven lifts:
A "Thank you God, for a' your gifts!"
Nae hymn by Angels could compare
Wi' this, a bairnie's bed-time prayer.

A bairnie sleeps. The night's begun;
But when tomorrow's risin' sun
Creeps up the sky tae stert the day,
A child will rise again tae play.

THE ONE-ARM BANDIT

(In reply to a newspaper article about a One-Arm Bandit
being installed in an Ayrshire pub once frequented
by Burns)

What's this I see afore my e'en?
Some hellish, heathen, Fruit Machine,
That spoils the image o' this scene,
    An' brings tae scorn
This haven o' my dearest freen',
    John Barleycorn.

What place hae you in Ayrshire's lore?
Who let you through this auld pub door?
Begone! An' ne'er be seen no more
    You ugly scunner!
Were you the whelp o' Satan's spore,
    I shouldna wunner!

Damned be the one designed your breed,
Tae prey on human weaknesses an' greed!
The love o' money is the creed
    On which you thrive.
The hard-earned coins on which you feed
    Keeps you alive.

When folks cam here tae cure their drouth,
They see your ever-open mooth,
That yawns in manner maist uncouth,
    Tae tempt each sinner.
For they believe, in very truth,
    They're oan a winner!

Tae sate your fiendish appetite,
Wi' every silver coin you bite,
The punters queue night efter night,
    Tae tempt their fate;
An' hopin' there's a chance you might
    Regurgitate!

It seems a shame that poor mankind
Are born sae gullible an' blind;
Could they but read your devious mind
    Frae you they'd run,
When they discover you're designed
    For gain – not fun!

Whatever wiles you may devise,
Tae tease an' cheat an' tantalise,
There is no way you can disguise
    Your base intent;
A fool frae his money's easy prised –
    As weel you kent!

Thank God there's some cam through the door
Who can your ugly sicht ignore,
Because your presence they deplore;
    An' you can take it,
Your ootstretched airm will be damned sore
    Afore I shake it!

HOMILY IN VERSE

Three men, who died on the self same day,
On their final journey made their way,
To meet before the Judgement Gate;
Awaiting their Eternal Fate.
And as they stood with eyes downcast –
Each with his dreams of a life now past –
They had not long to wait before
They saw, within the hallowed door,
An awesome figure dressed in white,
Surrounded by a brilliant light.
Not knowing from whence the creature came;
Not knowing his status or his name;
Yet each man knew in strict accord:
Here was an angel of The Lord!
The angel looked from face to face,
"What seek you in this Holy Place?
Your very presence here implies
You've come to claim your Paradise."

"I claim that right!" one man replied,
"For in my earthly life I've tried
To make the world a better place,
For all the people of my race.
I've tried in every way I can
To speak up for my fellow man!"

"Oh, yes," the angel said, "for some
Your name will live for years to come.
A politician of renown!
A man whose voice no one could drown!
A man who'd quickly silence those
Supporting schemes that he'd oppose!
In life you only had one aim;
A zest for power; a zest for fame!
No time to pause; no time to guess
The rising cost of your success.
To keep ahead in all men's eyes
You've stooped to intrigue and to lies;
You plotted, schemed, and cast aside
Your Truth, your Honesty, your Pride.
In countless ways to meet your ends
You've sacrificed your closest friends.
You may have fooled the human race,
But Politics here have little place!"

With that the angel turned his head
And to the second man he said,
"You too it seems can claim the right
To being a man of power and might,
With many servants close at hand
Awaiting on your next command."

"You speak the truth," the man replied,
"My wealth I never have denied.
The burning urge which I possess
To climb the ladder of success

Has put me where I yearned to be –
Among The Kings of Industry.
In every hour of every day
My factories work constantly
To meet the ever-growing demands
Of goods that bear my special brands,
I've built an Empire unsurpassed;
An Empire that will surely last.
And I take pride that I have made
Such impact on the world of trade!"

The angel raised his slender hand,
"I think," he said, "we understand.
The earthly goods which you possessed
Are products of a mind obsessed.
But all the things you seem to crave
You cannot take beyond the grave.
The treasure chests, you hold so dear,
What can that money buy you here?
The business empire you control;
Can it now save your mortal soul?
Is it not so, the things you cherish
Will fade away and quickly perish?
Even now, look back and see
That all your loving family
Are squabbling for the things you own;
Like jackals fighting for a bone!
In all your many well-planned schemes
To build the Empire of your dreams,
You had not time to lay much stress
On Everlasting Happiness.

You've turned your back on God, it's true.
Will he now do the same to you?"

The third man stood without a sound,
His eyes fixed firm upon the ground.
The angel looked on him and said,
"Come now, my friend, hold high your head.
You have no need to fret or fear,
For every soul must pass through here.
But first, I'm sure you know full well,
Each man has his own tale to tell."

The man was hesitant and meek,
A single tear rolled down his cheek,
"I have no wealth; I have no power,
To boast of in my final hour.
I've lived – as many others do –
With just enough to see me through.
I've had my share of joys and woes;
The good times and the body-blows.
I'm just an ordinary man,
Who's tried to do the best he can
On all the things I deem correct;
Like dignity and self-respect.
My life has been no great event,
But through it all I've been content."

The angel took him by the arm,
His smile was radiant and warm,

"My friend," he said, "it's plain to see
You are a man of modesty.
You make your life sound commonplace,
And yet, it's been a life of grace.
In every step along the road
Your Christian Faith has been the code.
You've clasped within your work-worn hands
The Holy Writ of God's commands.
The worthy standards you have set
Have long inspired all those you've met.
And one thing more we must recall,
Your greatest triumph of them all;
The one indeed which I am sure
Will make your place in Heaven secure.
Your saintly ways have surely won
A great vocation for your son;
And 'though your worldly life has ceased,
You've left on Earth a brand-new priest.
An ordinary man, you say?
I'd put it quite a different way!"

Three men who died on the self-same day
On their final journey made their way,
To meet before The Judgement Gate;
Awaiting their Eternal Fate . . .
The question is, how would you fare
Among the trio standing there?

THE ITHER SEX

At getherins we're a' inclined
Tae drink a Toast Tae Womankind,
But here tonight I have a mind
    My throat tae flex
An' speak aboot, in words refined,
    The Ither Sex.

'Though sprung we be frae Adam's rib,
Who is there that would dare tae crib,
That females hae become mair glib
    In ha'ein' their say;
There's little doubt that Women's Lib
    Is here to stay.

But ladies, as you a' weel ken,
You wad be loast withoot your men;
They pamper you; they ca' you "hen";
    It's nice tae hiv them.
At times they'll drive you roon' the ben' . . .
    But you'll forgive them!

In times o' stress can you deny
Their shoother is the place tae cry.
Besides, when in the bed you lie,
    The Lord be thankit,
They save you goin' oot tae buy
    A heated blanket.

They pay your rent; control the weans;
They dig the gairden; clean the drains;
At times they'll wash the windae panes;
    Or change a socket.
You're always free tae pick their brains . . .
    But no' their pocket!

There only is wan way tae thrive,
Tae keep this crazy world alive,
So, lads an' lassies, let us strive
    Tae be mair tender;
We need each ither tae survive –
    Whate'er the gender!

TO NANCY

Oh Nancy, lay thy haun' in mine;
That gentle haun' sae sweet,
An' let me brush my lips wi' thine,
My heart is at thy feet.

Then tae a land we'll baith awa';
A land o' bubblin' streams;
Where Hate's ne'er kent, and Love means a';
A land o' pleasant dreams.

Like sovereigns great we'll rule oor state.
Sich happiness we'll find;
For King an' Queen are man an' mate
In the kingdom o' the mind.

Oor laws will be the laws o' Love;
Nae laws were better founded.
We'll live on manna from above,
An' drink tae joys unbounded.

Oh Nancy, lay thy haun' in mine,
Oor lifelines clasped thegither,
An' airm-in-airm we'll ae find time
Tae care for yin anither.

EPITAPH OF FREEDOM

Beside the road a cairn stands,
Built by a thousand grateful hands,
Reminding all who pass this way
That Freedom's price is hard to pay.
There, carved in stane, for a' tae see
Are names that gave tae you an' me
The greatest gift a man can give —
They gave their lives that we might live.

But now they've passed tae legend lore,
Tae rank wi' heroes gone before;
In ageless realm they've found admission,
The Highland Fifty-first Division.

Who were these men who gained such fame,
From Flanders mud to Alamein?
Were they great warriors set apart;
Fanatics of a bluidy art,
Who marched and conquered; fought an' killed
That lust for power could be fulfilled?
A warlike race who'd flaunt their might,
And fought because they loved to fight?
Or, jealous o' some other nation,
They found in war their true vocation?

Naw! Those who formed The Fifty-first
For blood or war had little thirst.
They turned frae strife; despised aggression . . .
But, oh so much, they feared oppression
That when a tyrant's gory hand
Stretched oot tae snatch their native land,
They turned from peace and heard the cry
That called to Scotland "Fight or Die!"

They left their cattle on the hills;
They left their crofts; their whisky stills;
They left their factories and their shops;
They left their looms; they left their crops.
They came frae toon an' countryside –
The cream o' Scotland's manly pride –
Tae don the kilt an' tartan trews;
Tae swell the ranks an' spread the news,
That regiments famed in mony fights,
Were ready tae defend their rights.

Wi' prood Argylls they marched awa',
Or jined The Gallant Forty-twa;
In Aberdeen The Gordons grouped,
Frae other airts The Seaforths trooped;
In numbers fast The Camerons grew,
An' followed the pibroch o' Donald Dhu.

These were the men who left their all,
Tae answer Freedom's urgent call.

Their marching feet would never cease
'Til halted in an honest peace;
Then they'd return tae simple lives,
Tae sweethearts an' tae honest wives.
Thus was oor heritage preserved,
By loyal sons oor country served.
For foreign lands they left their hames
Right was their cause an' staunch their claims;
Brave was their heart, their spirits high
As proud they watched their colours fly;
For well they knew the flags they bore
Were steeped in history and in lore!

The prize was great but high the cost –
Sae mony comrades maimed or lost –
In the ebb and flow of battle's flood,
Swelled by a sea of Scottish blood.
Would Peace e'er walk the Earth again?
When would this maddened world turn sane?
For some it mattered now no more,
Their valiant fight for life was o'er!

Across the lands the battles raged,
Frae shore tae shore the troops engaged;
Times advancing; times retreating;
Tired an' worn – but never beaten!
Firm in their purpose tae defend,
'Til right – triumphant in the end! –
Gave them the victory they deserved;
The war was won! Peace was preserved!

Oor sojer lads came back once more
Tae start where they had left before;
Tae build what they had won wi' guns,
A fitting place tae raise their sons.
But, ever foremost in their mind,
They thought of those they'd left behind.

May gentle winds that fan the ground
Where lie those heroes, bring the sound,
The sound that they'd most love tae hear;
The pibroch sounding loud an' clear,
An' playin' their regiment's refrain
Tae tell them, "You died not in vain!"

STILL FLOWS THE BURNS

Appendix

INTRODUCTION

"Still Flows the Burns" is a volume of verse which aims at modernising some of the most popular poems of our National Bard. The basic idea can be carried to yet a further stage by utilising a number of poems from this book as the basis for a modern Burns Supper.

The information which follows outlines a tried and tested format for an evening of poetry and fun. The original entertainment from which the programme was derived was held in a small local hall. The two hundred guests attending were seated around the perimeter of a postage-stamp dance-floor, with a small platform at the top end. The dance-floor and the platform provided an adequate performing area for the cabaret entertainment following the meal.

The suggested programme may be readily curtailed or augmented depending on the facilities of the selected venue and the availability of local talent.

PROGRAMME

ITEM	REF.
CHAIRMAN'S INTRODUCTORY REMARKS	Note 1
THE IMMORTAL MEMORY – "A Toast To Rab" – Guest Speaker	Page 15
PIPING IN THE MEAL	Note 2
"TO A FISH SUPPER" – Guest Speaker	Page 29
THE MEAL	Note 3
SELECTION OF BURNS SONGS (3 Numbers) – Choir or Group	
HIGHLAND DANCER(S) – Two Dances	
SOLO SINGER – Two Burns Songs	
HIGHLAND DRESS – Audience Participation Game – Ladies Only	Note 4
TOAST TO THE LASSIES – Guest Singer/ Speaker with Choir or Group Backing	Note 5

(1) Green Grow the Rashes, O   Page 41
(2) The Lassies   Page 57

LINES SCRIBBLED – Various Guest Speakers   Note 6

WHISKY GALORE – Audience Participation
     Game – Men Only   Note 7

HIGHLAND DANCER(S) – Two Dances

SOLO SINGER – Two Burns Songs

"TAM THE BUNNET" – Guest Speaker   Page 19

QUOTES FROM RAB – Audience
     Participation Game – Mixed Couples   Note 8

BURNS SINGALONG – Choir or Group and
     Audience   Note 9

If time allows, the evening may end with dancing to some popular Scottish records.

The main purpose of the Chairman's Introductory Remarks, apart from welcoming everyone, is to brief the assembled guests on the type of entertainment ahead. His remarks should be along the lines . . . "Any true Scot will tell you that for the best of entertainment there's nothing like a real Burns Supper. Well, that's what we have for you tonight: NOTHING LIKE A REAL BURNS SUPPER!"

He continues by pointing out that the normal method used in a formal Burns Night is to travel back in time to the days when Burns was alive and well, and living in Ayrshire. Instead of this, they intend this evening to bring Rab forward to find out some of his views on life in the twentieth century.

He concludes his speech by introducing the guest speaker who will get the evening under way by proposing a Toast To The Immortal Memory – "A Toast To Rab", page 15.

The piper comes from the kitchen area followed by a guest speaker carrying a covered salver.

They parade the salver around the floor before the speaker takes up his position near the centre of the performing area, where he places the salver on a small table where a couple of glasses are already waiting. He hands one of the glasses to the piper who toasts the salver before departing.

The speaker now removes the cover from the salver to reveal a delicately wrapped fish supper in vinegar-stained newspaper. He gently opens the wrappings to reveal the precious contents as he recites his toast "To A Fish Supper", page 29.

NOTE 3 – THE MEAL

Immediately following the Toast To A Fish Supper, a team of willing helpers supply the guests with individually wrapped fish suppers (the result of prior negotiations with the local "chippie").

These fish suppers, on the advice of the Chairman, may be eaten directly from the paper (the only true way to enjoy such a banquet), or may be transferred to the paper plates provided on each table.

Tea, coffee and bread and butter may also be served to supplement the meal.

KILTIE CARD

SEE NOTE 4, PAGE 97

With the Compliments of

STILL *flows* THE BURNS

Prop List

– 4 obstacles for each contestant taking part. Empty beer cans are ideal for this purpose.
– 1 KILTIE CARD*, showing a Highlander without his kilt, for each contestant.
– 1 CUT-OUT KILT for each contestant.
– 1 BLINDFOLD for each contestant.

Method

This is the first of the Audience Participation Games in the programme and it is confined to ladies only. The compere or M.C. asks for lady volunteers from among the guests. Four or five is an ideal number. Having obtained the required number, the compere then goes on to explain that what they are about to do resembles the old party game "Pinning the Tail on the Donkey", but in this particular instance they will be "Putting the Kilt on the Scotsman". For this purpose the contestants are each given one of the tartan cut-out kilts which they hold with the adhesive side pointing outwards. The contestants are then positioned along the bottom end of the floor. Facing them, at the opposite end of the floor, are an equal number of assistants, each one holding a Kiltie Card. Spaced out along the respective "lanes" of each contestant are the four obstacles mentioned in the Prop List. The compere explains that the idea of these obstacles is to introduce an element of difficulty into the game, and if any of the obstacles are knocked over, the offending contestant is immediately eliminated. He then calls on the contestants to "Get set!"; then, in a most apologetic voice, he adds, "I'm sorry, but I almost forgot to tell you, you are blindfolded!" Each contestant is then blindfolded, and as the compere supposedly inspects each one to make sure they cannot see, the four obstacles are very quickly and very silently removed from each lane. The compere then gives the word to "Go", and the spectacle of the contestants moving forward very gingerly to avoid the invisible objects provides plenty of laughter. The eventual winner is, of course, the contestant who manages to stick the kilt nearest to the exact position, determined by the dotted line. They are rewarded with a small prize.

* The KILTIE CARDS and CUT-OUT KILTS may be easily made as follows:

(1) Graph up the line drawing of the little Scotsman to fit an A4 size paper.

(2) Photocopy number required and mount individually on stiff card.

(3) Trace kilt by following dotted line and cut out number required from light card.

(4) Cover front side of each cut-out kilt with tartan paper.

(5) Attach adhesive strips to opposite sides of cut-out kilts. Double-sided tape is ideal for this purpose as the protective cover can be left on until the last minute.

NOTE 5 – THE TOAST TO THE LASSIES

A mini-production number for this item on the programme can be easily arranged as follows. The guest speaker/singer takes up his position at the centre of the performing area. Behind him the choir or group is arranged to give their vocal support.

The speaker/singer sings solo each verse of the modernised version of "Green Grow the Rashes, O" to the tune of the original. Between each verse, the choir or group joins in the chorus.

Immediately following the final verse, the speaker/singer continues by reciting "The Lassies", page 57.

NOTE 6 – LINES SCRIBBLED

The duration of this item is very much left to the discretion of the organisers. It may be as long or as short as time allows. The various speakers involved should, however, be dressed in costumes relevant to their selected verses. The following examples are given for guidance only.

The compere introduces the item by pointing out that in his time Robert Burns is reputed to have scribbled rhymes on various objects which caught his fancy. The present day would, no doubt, have provided him with ample opportunities to continue this practice. He might, for example, have expressed these kind of thoughts on seeing a C.N.D. poster . . .

ENTER A BEATNIK TYPE CHARACTER, COMPLETE WITH DUFFLE COAT, THREADBARE JEANS, BARE FEET AND OPEN SANDALS AND CARRYING A "BAN THE BOMB" BANNER. HE RECITES POEM ON PAGE 53 AND MAKES HIS WAY OFF.

COMPERE: On the other hand his inspiration could be derived on viewing the tombstone of a dead Celt . . .

ENTER PALE FIGURE DRESSED IN CELTIC FOOTBALL STRIP WITH ANGELIC WINGS ATTACHED TO THE BACK. HE RECITES POEM ON PAGE 52.

The chapter on LINES SCRIBBLED . . . provides a number of opportunities to continue this programme item as desired.

Prop List

A tray containing five small glasses. Four of the glasses hold an equal measure of fake whisky – which is in reality cold tea.

The fifth glass holds an equal measure of genuine whisky.

All of the glasses are covered with cling film so that no tell-tale aroma betrays the real thing.

Method

It is now the turn of men only to join in another Audience Participation Game.

The compere recruits six male volunteers from the assembled guests. Five of these he lines up along the top end of the performing area. The sixth man is placed in a position where he can view the facial expressions of the five others.

The compere passes along the line with the tray of glasses informing the contestants that they must select a glass, but must not remove the cover. When each man has his glass, the compere goes on to explain that every true Scot should be able to recognise good whisky, but, in fact, only one of the contestants is holding the real thing. To add to the agony, he explains one of the glasses contains only cold tea; another contains your other national drink, made from girders; another glass is holding a very strong laxative; while a fourth glass will keep everyone guessing – not what it is, but whose it is!

The compere now tells the drinkers that when he gives the word they must whip off the cover and down their drink at one go. They must then remain stationery . . . all except the one who has taken the laxative. He then tells the sixth man to watch their faces and see if he can spot the one who has just swallowed the real whisky.

The compere is now ready to give the word of command. The five contestants swallow their drinks. The sixth contestant must now make his decision. Before he does so, the compere tells him he will allow him to ask each contestant one question, but he must understand that only the contestant who selected the real whisky must tell the truth; the other four can lie. The questions are asked; the answers are given; and Mr Number 6 makes his selection. The compere then requests the real whisky drinker to take one pace forward. If the sixth contestant has guessed correctly, he is awarded a prize; if he is incorrect, the prize goes to the man who has just stepped forward.

Prop List

The following are required for each couple taking part.

A tray or small table with these articles:

– False dentures – from the local joke shop
– Small haggis
– A mouse – chocolate or sugar from sweet shop
– Tam o' Shanter bonnet
– A rose – artificial or real

Also required for each couple, a writing pad and pen.

Method

The final Audience Participation Game is for mixed couples. The number of couples taking part may be 2, 3 or 4 depending on the availability of the required props.

The ladies are each given a writing pad and pen and take up their positions across the top end of the performing area facing the assembled guests. Their respective gentlemen partners are positioned a few steps behind next to a tray or table containing the array of articles as indicated in the Prop List.

The compere now explains that what he is about to do is read out a selection of quotes from well known Burns poems. After each quote the ladies will require to write down the title of the poem from which the lines are taken; while their male partners require to hold up the correct article relating to that particular poem.

Points are awarded after each quote; two points for a correct title and two points for a correct article. The eventual winners are, of course, the couple with the highest points total.

Quotes

(1) I'm truly sorry man's dominion,
   Has broken nature's social union.

   ANSWER: TO A MOUSE

(2) Till a' the seas gang dry, my Dear
   And rocks melt wi' the sun

   ANSWER: MY LOVE IS LIKE A RED, RED ROSE

(3) But pleasures are like poppies spread
   You seize the flow'r, its bloom is shed

   ANSWER: TAM O' SHANTER

(4) Fair fa' your honest, sonsie face,
    Great chieftain o' the puddin-race!

ANSWER: ADDRESS TO A HAGGIS

(5) But thee – thou hell o' a' diseases –

ANSWER: ADDRESS TO THE TOOTHACHE

To end the night a chance for all to join in the show; a medley of popular Burns songs with the choir or group leading the community singing.

An even more enthusiastic response will result if printed song sheets are distributed among the guests.

The following are the type of songs which always appeal:

YE BANKS AND BRAES
MY LOVE IS LIKE A RED, RED ROSE
COMIN' THRO' THE RYE
SCOTS WHA HAE
AULD LANG SYNE

THE LAST WORD . . .

An essential facility of any Burns Night – traditional or otherwise – is The Bar.

Make sure that whatever you do the evening's entertainment is punctuated with opportunities for the guests to replenish their glasses.

As mentioned at the start, NOTHING LIKE A REAL BURNS NIGHT; but nevertheless the kind of night that Rab himself would really have enjoyed; a night of fun and games; a night of poetry and song; a night when the Chairman can get to his feet and say with sincerity:

> My freens the honour fa's tae me
> Tae thank oor gracious company,
> For a' the wond'rous harmony
>   That we hae shared.
> For nichts like this, I pray that we
>   May lang be spared.

Hugh J. Waters was born in Barrhead, Renfrew-
shire, in 1926. Disabled from birth, he has
nevertheless enjoyed a full and active life.
Married with three children, he retired in 1987
after 30 years employment with S.T.V. as a
television scriptwriter.